AF265939

Far In The Meadows

AND OTHER POEMS

Far In The Meadows

And Other Poems

Meenakshi Raina

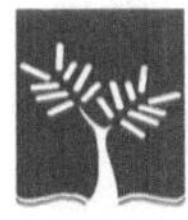

TAMARIND TREE BOOKS
Toronto

Copyright © 2019: Meenakshi Raina

All rights reserved. No part of this publication may be reproduced, stored in a retrieval system or transmitted in any form or by any means (electronic, mechanical, photocopying, recording or otherwise) without the prior written permission of the publisher or the copyright owner. Inquiries should be addressed to:

Tamarind Tree Books Inc.,
14 Ferncastle Crescent,
Brampton, Ontario. L7A 3P2, Canada.
OR
Meenakshi Raina,
meenakshiraina@hotmail.com

Library and Archives Canada Cataloguing in Publication

Raina, Meenakshi, author
Far in the meadows : and other poems
/ Meenakshi Raina.

ISBN 978-0-9950538-9-2 (softcover)

I. Title.

PS8635.A4285F37 2018   C811'.6   C2018-905764-5

This book is dedicated to my parents
J.N Bhatt and Usha Kashkari

THE MAYOR AND MEMBERS OF COUNCIL
FOR
THE CITY OF MARKHAM

extend **Congratulations** *to*

MEENAKSHI RAINA

as you launch a

Poetry Collection

"Far in the Meadows"

December 2018

Frank Scarpitti
Mayor

Meenakshi Raina

CONTENTS

Contents

Contents

Contents

POET'S NOTE

Writing poems is my passion and over the last four years I have collected a treasure of more than two-hundred poems, verses and songs. My poetry is based on observation, imagination and personal experiences. I believe with just limited words a lot can be said and words have the power to comfort and bring hope.

'*Far In The Meadows and other poems*' – is a collection of selected ninety poems that revolve around three segments - Love, Life and Longing.

My hybrid identity as an Indo-Canadian creates a unique fusion of imagery from far East and West lands. These poems are an attempt to bring the trials and tribulations, nature and beauty, love and loss in one spectrum. Readers will experience a rollercoaster ride full of emotions and lessons from life.

There are poems that bring hope and delight along with the poems that confront pain and endless longing. Conventional rhyme, free verse and numerous other styles of poetry are woven together to create a variety for readers. Different facets that life has to offer can be seen on a literary landscape and I am sure it would appeal to all the readers in general and poetry lovers in particular.

This collection of poems will be my second publication after the historical fiction –'The Divine And The Destiny', which was published by Leadstart (India) in 2013 and the book was launched by the Bollywood actor Anupam Kher.

Let my poetry echo my thoughts. Happy reading!

Meenakshi Raina
December, 2018. Toronto.

{01} *Far In The Meadows*

Far in the meadows, below the vast sky,
I opened my arms and let ego fly,
From all rusted regrets and every grief,
In nature's lap I embraced pure relief,
Wandering butterflies tickled my toes,
I smiled and giggled, far in the meadows.

The rising sun with magnificent looks,
I cherished velvet voice of running brooks,
Once ugly anguish melted in sunlight,
My heart's empty room dazzled with delight,
I touched dancing dandelions in rows,
So splendid was I, far in the meadows.

When worried winds whisked my soul again,
Like worthless weeds, wilted my hidden pain,
Tangled in fast paced era of machines,
My life went deprived of beautiful scenes,
Burdened and haunted by unseen shadows,
I conquered my fears, far in the meadows.

While thin leaves of grass let fall beads of dew,
Beyond the hills at guard chirping birds flew,
Beauty of morning so pure and serene,
I blinked my eager eyes, it felt like dream,
Tossed the troubled thoughts, forgot wild woes,
I found inner peace, far in the meadows.

{02} *Life Is Fusion*

Think no past, it is now gone,
There is no time to rest and sit,
    Hold on to dreams and move on,
    And life is what we make of it.

If you wish for better future,
Act in present for pleasant time,
    Sow seeds of hope with labour,
    And learn to make your life sublime.

Only the dead believe in sleep,
While others combat in life,
    As they have promises to keep,
    And work hard to end their strife.

Life is fusion of sun and rain,
Clouds of sadness won't last long,
    Let the time heal all your pain,
    And turn life to easy song.

Cherish what you have with you,
Cry not for what you do not,
    Fortunate like you are very few,
    And thank God for what you got.

{Contd.} *Life Is Fusion*

Let not be conquered by woes,
Leave inner fears and march ahead,
    The fears you own are your foes,
    Secrets of future are unsaid.

Life is short to hold bitterness,
For your good, you learn to forgive,
    Bring smiles with your kindness,
    Death is the end, deeds shall live.

{03} *Rise Above It*

Keep no expectations from others,
be like a tree that even supports the branches
those do not bear any fruit.
Rise above the worldly expectations.

Those who envy and criticise,
maybe they are unsuccessful, with unpleasant past
and that reflects in their thoughts.
Rise above annoyance, just ignore them.

World is not only made of saints,
some may pronounce you are inferior to them
don't let them persuade you.
Rise above their influence, stay positive.

When things go wrong, don't blame others,
take some time to ponder to know what differently
things could have been done.
Rise above, learn from your mistakes.

Your fears are your biggest enemies,
fear of failure keeps you away from success
don't let fears conquer your heart.
Rise above, and overcome your freaky fears.

{Contd.} *Rise Above It*

Keep no grudges as life is too short,
forgiveness brings peace of mind or forget the
mistake and move forward.
Rise above those growing grudges.

Meenakshi Raina

{04} *Caves Of Sorrow*

In my dark deep caves of sorrow
I have the walls painted with tears,
Lonely I stand there with no hope
Tormented with unwanted fears.

Restless regrets roam and reside
In my dark deep caves of sorrow,
I exist as withered autumn
There is no spring for tomorrow.

Roses, reminded me of you
Now uprooted since you were gone,
In my dark deep caves of sorrow
My life is caged has not moved on.

With broken heart I feel disturbed
Some peace I wish, I could borrow,
Ashes of faith are now buried
In my dark deep caves of sorrow.

{05} *How Can I Sleep....*

How can I sleep with lot of fears?
I close my eyes to drop the tears,
How can I sleep with hungry mind,
Why peace in world is hard to find?
Values lost, selfish are prayers.

Why a fake smile everyone wears?
Kindness forgotten, no one cares,
Humanity, close to get blind.
How can I sleep?

Innocent die, fill earth's layers,
Leaving behind their grieving dears,
When shall evil spirits unwind?
I hope we can still save mankind,
Events of day and darkness scares.
How can I sleep?

{06} *Dusk And Dawn*

sunset spins sad sky
in raging red and crimson
the
fireball waves goodbye

birds fly to their nest
a tiresome day ends at dusk
and
night fills with moonlight

smiling stars appear
nude night dresses in calmness
while
wind murmurs to moon

new day born at dawn
sunshine brightens lonely sky
and
new hopes come to life.

{07} *Blessed I Am...*

Bullets and blood,
And people are dead,
There are many,
Who live in fear,
There are children,
Without any care,
Devils are on run,
Chasing the innocent.
Who knows when,
Life becomes a curse,
Tears have dried,
Smiles are forgotten,
Happiness is lost,
Humanity has frozen,
When I see,
World around me,
I realize how blessed I am,
To be with my loved ones.

{08} *Dreams*

Dreams are dreams,
Possibilities to discover,
A cherished desire,
A wish for the future,
An aspiration, a goal,
That stirs mind and soul.

Believe in your dreams,
Feel their power,
Dreams are the hopes,
That inspire to achieve,
And whisk you away,
On a colourful journey.

Pull dreams out of cradle,
Slowly let them grow,
Hold them, make them walk,
And strive to raise them,
It can happen, they may fall,
But every step is vital.

Relentless you shall be,
And nurture them again,
Make them stronger,
Stronger than before,
Certainly they will be,
A reality of your life.

For anyone who dreams,
Dreams to bring a change,
Remember the change,
That you see today,
Was someone's dream,
A dream in yesterday.

{09} *Love*

Love me endless, like sapphire sky,
 Give me the silver stars of delight,
And I shall be your beloved bride,
 I pledge in ideal ivory moonlight.

Let your emerald caring multiply,
 And evolve in pious carnation love,
Let your saffron devotion spellbind,
 And I shall honour it with bow.

Blend your sensuous soul with mine,
 Let our bistre shadows be seen one,
Amaze me with the love I long for,
 And leave me with regrets none.

Love me, not for my lilac loveliness,
 With passing time it shall wither,
Love me, not for my marigold smile,
 But, bestow me altruistic love forever.

For rest of my life's journey ahead,
 Love me, conquer my crimson heart,
And cradle me in your arms my love,
 Nothing but unkind death shall us part.

{10} *Wailing*

no one knows nothing
when wrapped with
smooth silver silence
some secrets sleep.

helpless heart hopes
love lives long
but beneath betrayal
deep desires die.

time twists tides
some sail safe
some seize sand
while wailing waiting.

{11} *I Want To Be...*

Mystic moon gazed inside the room,
Diminished the darkness of night,
Wet winds, embraced never before,
And I woke up, calm and quiet.
While I slept like untroubled child,
She had been awake all night long,
Speechless was I, and tried to muse,
Who made her different and strong?
Volcanic heat peaked in my veins,
Motionless, I laid ailing in bed,
She squeezed a small wet cloth,
That rested to cool my forehead.

Heaven in her eyes, I got to see,
She is the woman I want to be.

Silent and soft, I felt her touch,
My head sunk deep in pillow,
She watched gathering her silence,
And let her tears, completely flow.
While she adored more than before,
I utterly forgot the merciless pain,
To honour her love and discomfort,
I closed my eyes once again.
A journey then began in my head,
And thoughts swamped like a storm,
Only time had she smiled, at my cry,
Must be the day I was born.

Meenakshi Raina

{Contd.} *I Want To Be...*

In my thoughts, I prayed to Almighty,
She is the woman I want to be.

Some things that she couldn't give,
Maybe for lack of time or money,
A sad account that I held, met end,
Her selfless love brought serenity.
Seeds of virtues she had nurtured,
Without them, life wouldn't be bright,
I learnt to make my life sublime,
And, set apart my imprisoned pride.
If I could ever peep in her heart,
Nothing but love, I would find,
And her heart would keep saying,
"You shall always be my child".

Her heart is now a shrine to me,
She is the woman I want to be.

Different shades of grey, appeared,
Were not just aging marks by time,
But modesty grown to its pinnacle,
That made her elegant and sublime.
Though time swallowed her youth,
A pretty woman she had been,
Despite wrinkles, her face glowed,
And endless beauty she held within.
A simple but happy life she lived,

{Contd.} *I Want To Be...*

She grew in age and love together,
I found blend of truth and beauty,
And innocence utterly like flower.

I too want a life cage free,
She is the woman I want to be.

As I scrolled through old days,
Some tough times she had seen,
Have no words to praise her valour,
A pillar of strength she had been.
Not rich, not famous, not a super-star,
I want to be her true reflection,
Was it, what she desired to make of me?
With heart of gold- a complete woman.
Words of wisdom, I gained from her,
Sense of spirituality she bestowed,
For eternal peace and solace,
When she prayed, I too followed.

Yes, she is so divine to me,
She is the woman I want to be.

She guarded like a medieval knight,
And the night of unrest did traverse,
None but her, shall I place my trust,
Eternal shall be her love, in my verse.
Early morning bells were heard,

{Contd.} *I Want To Be...*

And my chain of thoughts ended,
She turned on me her quiet eyes,
And smiled and kissed, contented.
The day returned and night was done,
Windows waited for sun rays to enter,
Relieved of pain, I gazed at her,
And thanked my fate for loving mother.

My inner voice kept telling me,
She is the woman I want to be.

{12} *Last Goodbye*

I waited again for you, until sunset,
You had promised, you would come,
Abandoned sea and cloudless sky,
Was a perfect day to spend together.

Now I know you will never come,
For you I wrote, last goodbye on sand,
It too shall be washed by roaring tides,
And you will never know, I was there.

How shall I mute memories of you,
There aren't many but there are few,
Where do I mend my broken heart,
I wish we were together and not apart.

II

I wasn't rich enough to be handsome,
Your father told me two days before,
Now I shall dwell in an unknown land,
But I kept my promise, visited the shore.

When you left, I gazed at the vacant sea,
I touched your goodbye, on wet sand,
You will never know, it wasn't the tide,
But me, who wiped it, with sorrow hand.

{13} *Optimistic Orange*

Let the night embrace you with honey dreams,
Where you find your beloved dressed in tangerine,
She promises love and you kiss her marmalade lips,
The trust you longed for, in her titian eyes is seen.

In the saffron valley where good things happen,
She sings to heal all your inner rustic wounds,
She offers you sip, from coral river of happiness,
And you believe her and listen to salmon sounds.

With bright orange sunshine, new day begins,
You hope someday, your orange lady you will find,
Your heart blooms like the young marigold,
Life seems beautiful, amber fears are left behind.

{14} *My Homeland Kashmir*

I yearn to go back to my home; I left two decades ago,
I closed my eyes and let my mind wander in my home,
I found rooms with no doors, air so stale and lifeless,
Everything so dark, filled with dust and crazy cobwebs,
I stumbled, got back control; found some small stones,
I saw few beehives dangling with no bees around,
Dead birds lying silent and some had left their bones.

I thought of my childhood, spent behind those walls,
Kitchen, where mother cooked appeared dungeon now,
Somehow tap was still there, waiting for water to flow,
It was hard to believe, life existed there two decades ago,
Broken, eaten by termites, was every piece of furniture,
I heard the window slap, now open for years together,
Sunlight peeped through, and I got the horrific picture.

I opened my eyes, sorrow pinched me, eyes held tears,
Memories of brutal past haunted me all those years,
Chased with guns, I was hounded from my homeland,
Frightened, I ran for life and then I never returned,
Time no more bothers me as I have waited too long,
I yearn for peace, when shall I return to my land?
Echoes from past scare me, but I hope to stay strong.

{15} *Hope*

Every new morning brings me hope,
Someday peace and happiness will prevail.
Present is spent in shaping our future,
Our efforts for peace shall never fail.

Let us share a common dream,
Let us rise together to weed out the foe.
Unity is strength and shall always be,
The seeds of love for sure will grow.

For our future generations that come,
Let us make the world a safe place.
We have one life to live on,
Let us live with dignity and grace.

Let the endless power of the Divine,
Help us on our way.
For peace and happiness of all,
Let us all, together pray.

{16} *Your Letters*

Love hurts, brings pain,
I never knew before.
You walked away unsaid,
I waited more and more.

Today I threw away,
Your letters written in blue.
I won't see them again,
They reminded me of you.

You left so many questions,
Answers, I couldn't find.
Everything is now clean,
My drawer and my mind.

Regrets have now faded,
Life has moved on.
It is over a year now,
Since you were gone.

{17} *Shades Of Emerald*

Shall I compare you to colour green,
As harmony of Nature, in you is seen.

I confuse your smile with green spring,
While both bring mystic delight to me,
You hold calmness of green meadows,
And carry elegance of humble palm trees.

You have embraced the youthfulness,
Which follows the beautiful evergreen,
All my green wounds, are now healed,
You sincerely made my life serene.

You are untainted, your heart so pure,
Like the zesty wine from green grapes,
I owe you, the greenery in my life,
Shades of emerald you get to my paradise.

{18} Seashore

With my eyes closed,
I lay near the shore,
Lips of tide gave wet kiss,
I felt the eternal bliss.

My anger melted in sun,
I let myself sink in sand,
While eyes stared at sea,
I tried to set my mind free.

Calm winds passed by,
And blew away my regrets,
I laughed loud and smiled,
I felt like innocent child.

When I need to unwind,
I will come back to the shore,
It had changed enough of me,
Far away, I still hear the sea.

{19} *Forever In Your eyes*

First time as I met your
eyes, found them gateway
to your heart
Observing them I was
mesmerized, it was not easy
to look apart
Rejoiced my gaze and I
have to confess, it was love
at first sight
Everlasting memories eyes
did create, in silent and
starry night
Voiceless was I, my heart
raced while I tried to
unlock my gaze
Enticed by your eyes, I
conceded to be lost in an
endless maze
Regrets from life melted
away, and I forgot my old
doleful days

In the years gone by,
though youth is lost but
our love has grown
Nestled in love's warmth
secrets of my heart your
eyes have known

Your miraculous eyes are
so sincere, they don't know
how to lie
Ocean of love for you I feel,
you shall stay in my heart
until I die
Unforgettable is our past,
beautiful years we have
spent together
Refreshed are those
memories, filled with
happiness and laughter

Even today when I look at
your eyes I sail deep and
get immersed
Your eyes, so intoxicating,
I find them perfect for my
poetic verse
Everlasting is my love for
you, you came as a blessing
in disguise
Seal your eyes for sleep
now, when they open, it
will be my sunrise.

{20} Soldier's Beloved

Let me compare you with seasons,
When I wait for you, it feels spring,
Like buds waiting to bloom and,
Meadows keen to turn green,
My inner spring brings hope in me,
That soon together we shall be.

When we meet, it is like summer,
Life is beautiful, a bright sunshine,
Precious moments shared together,
Are filled with love and laughter,
If things are real, sometimes I think,
I pinch myself and try to blink.

It is hard to be, a soldier's beloved,
When you leave, my smiles are gone,
My autumn arrives, I feel withered,
And with a heavy heart, we part,
But I know, you have to go,
Defend the land and fight the foe.

{Contd.} *Soldier's Beloved*

When you are far away from me,
I am silent like winter snow,
And the gusty winds of loneliness,
Remind your love and tenderness,
Your absence is filled by memories,
I think of you and write in my diaries.

This is how I feel for you and,
My seasons are altogether different,
Although people say it is summer,
But my summer hasn't yet arrived,
You often visit me in my dreams,
And you miss me too it seems.

{21} Friday Thirteen

Yes, they too believed in love,
Yet became victims of hate,
Men hungry for destruction,
And with vicious mindset,
Fired deadly bullets around,
Lifeless bodies fell on ground.

Pain touched every heart,
For some, life won't be same,
Laughter transformed to cries,
Happiness changed to grief,
Merciless sinners did it all,
At concert, cafe and football.

Flesh and blood piled on roads,
Obedient bodies stayed silent,
Many were counted dead,
Others were counted wounded,
And some waited for last breath,
Paris mourned the gruesome death.

{22} Carved Hearts

At the footbridge she always read his name
along with hers that they had carved together
on the wooden side plank.
They also had carved two hearts intertwined,
though their love met an early end she still
meets him in her dreams.
When she passes the bridge it brings back
those golden memories when they walked
together hand in hand.
She still watches the pair of swans passing
under the footbridge and feels his presence
somewhere around watching.
When soft snow covers the carving, she wipes
off the snow to make his name visible and
kisses it with her cold lips.
Whenever she feels lonely, she comes to the
footbridge, it is now like a shrine to her
after his untimely death.

{23} *Sharp Words*

Sharp words leave invisible scars, and pain,
They pierce like sword and harm the soul.
Such painful words keep echoing the ears,
With no scope left for the heart to console.

Like arrows sharp words hurt deep inside,
Though their wounds are not visible to eyes.
Time may heal them but scars stay forever,
Watch your words before it is late to realize.

Love and bonding gets created over years,
But sharp words split relationship so quick.
Like a mirror broken into thousand pieces,
So don't throw your sharp words as a brick.

{24} *Life In Exile*

When innocent got killed, others left,
Beyond the hills to unknown lands,
Escaping death that chased foot prints,
With nothing, just the empty hands.

Helpless Pandits, became homeless,
Feet on ground and sky over head,
Horror and fear gripped their minds,
Their heart was alive but soul so dead.

Loaded guns, kept looking for them,
The torment they couldn't withstand,
And even in sleep, they would weep,
As they dreamt of their native land.

Empty tents, to call their new home,
At times blew away in wind and cold,
Years went on, in absolute darkness,
Many shattering stories never got told.

Nothing has changed culprits are free,
Tears have dried in twenty-nine years,
With no return, life in exile goes on,
Still the bitter past, haunts and scares.

**Pandits are the aboriginal minority of Kashmir (India). Kashmir, God's own land on earth, is the motherland of Kashmiri Pandits. The year 1990, saw a mass exodus of Kashmiri Pandits from their own soil due to threat to their life and, brutal and barbaric killings by the separatists. More than 400,000 Kashmiri Pandits were forced to abandon their homeland. Even today after twenty-nine years of their mass exodus, their ordeal continues....*

{25 } *Utopian Land*

My poetry takes me to Utopian land,
  Where love and peace perfectly blend.
   Humanity is the only religion known,
    Arrows are rusted, bows can't bend.

Everyone is kind with beautiful heart,
  Equality and justice for all, I wonder.
   A perfect place where women are safe,
    And it rains, without any thunder.

I imagine people living their dreams,
  Society woven from threads of trust.
   Here life is perfect, devils are dead,
    Joy prevails, worries crushed to dust.

But, when I encounter the real world,
  My poetic soap bubble tends to burst.
   And I am drawn out of Utopian land,
    Now I find blood quenching the thirst.

{26} *Solitude*

When wrapped in solitude,
I can imagine and dream,
Quietly, I allow myself,
To hear my inner soul.

Silence creeps in my heart,
And cures the old wounds,
It permits me to ponder,
And heals me from within.

False promises, fake smiles,
I find easy to recognize,
I feel the power of solitude,
It connects me with myself.

{27} *Our Love Is Cursed*

Such wondrous beauty held in eyes divine,
I wish this lovely night would stay, be kind,
So blissful are her eyes, I need no wine,
Nothing to match her beauty can I find.

The morning sun shall take away the night,
And I shall wait till moon and stars arrive,
In darkness our love hides, so harsh the light;
Our love is cursed while unsought rivals thrive.

But, when we die, forever we shall sleep,
With unseen wings we leave, fly like a dove,
Our bodies, left in ground, cruel could keep;
We'll leave all things behind except our love.

Now wait for death to mix in dust and sand,
And hope we two unite in God's own land.

{28} *Dust*

In the dust of wicked worries,
    we are lost; find no time to live,
In the dust of obstinate ego,
    we find hard, to help and give.

In the dust of rusty resentment,
    we are left, with no peace within,
In the dust of regrets from past,
    we put laughter and smile, in bin.

Find time and dust off your mind,
    be vigorous, stronger than before,
Or else, happiness is hard to find,
    if dust is piled, in mind's store.

{29} *Ecstasy*

Entranced with my love for writing poetry, I
can be what I must be and the desire for
self-actualization makes my life purposeful.
To feel inspired, transformed and transcend is
a beautiful experience leading to intense joy.
Some might not understand what poetry is to me
yes, my ecstasy is hidden in the verses I write.

{30} *Emotions*

Endless sea of feelings
  Echo straight from the heart
    Endorse joy and sorrow
      Evolve as tears when sad
        Emerge as smile when glad
          Engage the five senses
            Empower mind and soul

{31} *Autumn Fire*

Afraid are the fragile leaves of fall,
  Unknown wind swirled and swept them all.
    The carpet of leaves in ginger, yellow and red,
      Under the trees they lay beautifully spread.
        Modest and silent stand the bare trees,
          Numbed and wondering how time flees.

First golden, then auburn turns the ground,
  Intense is glow of fire in all colors around.
    Red stands out, where as bronze is brilliant,
      Even orange shade looks bright and elegant.

{32} *Sleeping Wounds*

Crispiness of the morning breeze,
Woke up slumbering leaves on trees,
And I walked beside my loneliness,
To get some peace and serenity.

As sun brightened and day was ripe,
Slowly my pretence got peeled away,
I became aware of my sleeping wounds,
Buried in my heart's secret chamber.

Though I had stopped visiting my past,
But time didn't heal all my wounds,
With some it made no difference,
The amount of time that had gone by.

Wounds are those withered leaves,
Wailing on ground, around the trees,
Some are embraced by the wind,
While others stay long, to be a fossil.

{33} *The Opalescent Spring*

O Spring, come spread smile,
    frozen days will turn bright,
Buds will peep in unique style,
    birds shall chirp with delight.

With scary sky, dull and grey,
    winter was all white and wet,
For your eternal beauty, I pray,
    with warm days, ideal sunset.

Cherry blossom, won't be far,
    maple leaves will appear soon,
Greenery will fill-up, soil's scar,
    and stars will shine like moon.

Tulips shall dance with daffodils,
    butterflies will be fluttering,
Nature owns, magnificent skills,
    hurry up my opalescent spring.

Meenakshi Raina

{34} *All Over Again*

We have altered,
Yet pretend to be same,
Let us fall in love,
All over again.

Let us try rewind,
Memories left behind,
When my silence,
Reflected a lot,
And your mind,
Pursued my thought.

A simple hug from you,
Meant eternal bliss,
And you felt my eyes,
Enough to mesmerise,
We did share laughter,
And we did share cries.

When we walked on sand,
You held my hand,
We loved the open sky,
And watched the sunset,
Our love was so pure,
Filled with joy and zest.

Now we talk less,
Chat more on net,
And we have adapted,
To the concrete walls,
We did rise in life,
Our love suffered falls.

Let us find things we did,
From our memory lane,
So let us fall in love,
All over again.

{35} *Your Mystic Love*

Your mystic love conquered my heart
Life is beautiful, I never knew before
You gave me hope and a desire to live
Grievances from past weren't anymore.

Many seasons went by, since you left
You promised, I waited for your return
In loneliness, your memories haunt
And my broken heart can't stop to yearn.

Now my hope is completely shattered
All the little pieces of hope are in silent tears
Death alone can save from clutches of pain
I have waited enough for all these years.

Meenakshi Raina

{36} *Tomorrow Is Unknown*

Let the wheels of time ease,
Let the friendly night freeze.

Together we seize the moment
won't let it slip away.
Tomorrow is unknown for us
so I want you to stay.

My restless heart silently listens
to the rhythm of our love.
And this moment is all we have
with us right now.

Let the wheels of time ease,
Let the friendly night freeze.

The curtains of time are down
and it is just you and me.
We got this beautiful moment
planned by destiny.

Melt in this moment and think
there is no tomorrow.
I want to give you my smile and
take away your sorrow.

Let the wheels of time ease,
Let the friendly night freeze.

{37} *Walls Of Silence*

To me, a silent stranger, you've become,
Please talk to me, help keep our love alive.
This bitter quiet leaves affection numb,
With walls of silence love can not survive.

We prayed our wondrous love would never end,
Recall our fun and laughter in the rain.
I'll never let those memories descend,
Your haunting silence now drives me insane.

Let's now forgive mistakes of long ago,
Fly from the sad confines of loneliness.
Break down these walls of silence, let love grow,
I yearn for yesterday's togetherness.

You are my only love, to this I swear,
But walls of silence leave me cold and bare.

{38} *Autumn Breeze*

The shades of autumn, beautiful to see,
And I hear your whisper from fallen leaves,
I wish you could come, to be here with me,
So lonely and cold is the autumn breeze.

I miss your smile your joyful summer songs,
And I look for you in old memories,
I wish you were here, to enjoy the fall,
So lonely and cold is the autumn breeze.

Red and gold leaves, circle above the ground,
While sobbing and silent stand the bare trees,
I wish you could come, and sit beside me,
So lonely and cold is the autumn breeze.

{39} *Night Of Hunger*

In broken words she sang him lullaby,
 And tried to comfort him but he still cried,
  He could not sleep with wet eyes and lips dry,
   New night of hunger, for them had arrived,
    And she no more could hide her tears and wiped,
     Fate left her wander in deserted street,
      Troubled by hunger and tortured by heat,
       Homeless she was, after her husband's death,
        She smiled, held her child close to her heartbeat,
         While both counted stars, waited for last breath.

{40} *Notebook*

I possess a notebook, real reflection of my soul,
two decades plus five beautiful years of company.
When I turn the pages, memories are dusted off,
filled with poetic words, no empty pages I see.

A true testimony to the journey of my life,
with feelings and thoughts captured in lyrical way.
A place where shadow of my past resides,
and some scribbled lines never erased, still stay.

Pages have turned pale, bowed as autumn leaves,
and cardboard cover too tired to hold the pages.
Though it has lost its lustre, still precious to me,
I believe with time, the notebook too ages.

{41} *Even The Angels Wept*

Her country a war zone, where death was the king,
She held her baby in arms, left for unknown land,
Followed the crowd, and walked miles after miles,
Hunger and thirst became curse, couldn't withstand.

Her baby cried, closed his eyes, she felt his last breath,
She walked with the dead baby in her arms and wept,
When her limbs couldn't bear the weight of the dead,
She gave him a sand burial, forever her child slept.

So distressed and helpless, tears rolled from her eyes,
She knew she would never return to her child's grave,
With dead heart, she silently left followed the crowd,
Even the angels wept, they no more pretended brave.

* *In August 2014, attack by the separatists on Yazidis in Sinjar, Iraq, was a massacre. Fleeing civil war, there were hundreds of thousands running toward the mountain. Many of the men were killed, small children, the sick and elderly were carried until their relatives collapsed from exhaustion. People died of thirst, and there was no food or water. Corpses were left on the roadside, unburied. Mothers had to leave their babies behind.*

{42} Dark And Grey

When wise winds whispered
touched the tall tree tops,
branches opened like arms
to welcome the silent snow.
    Night was all dark and grey,
    moon buried in loneliness,
    rugged roads remained restless,
    while wild winds whipped.
In the night's silence I slipped
into a dream where you amazed
me with a sensuous sweet song
and secretly soothed my soul.

{43} *Legacy*

The past is already buried,
The precious present is gold,
Who knows what future holds,
Secrets of destiny are untold.

If you plant good thoughts,
It will lead to good deeds,
The poisonous fruits grow,
Only from poisonous seeds.

We are just sheer souls,
The dead people of future,
And the body we admire,
Shall blend in dust of Nature.

So, leave behind a legacy,
Be an example for the rest,
Why not use life wisely,
And use it to the best.

{44} *Wandering Winds*

Captured in calm castle of clouds,
    Invisible, incredible, infinite am I,
Whining wandering winds whisk,
    Sensuous and sensitive satin sky.

I wiggle willows in wilderness,
    Dance in circles with fallen leaves,
Filch fragrance from fine flowers,
    I fascinate with my bare breeze.

I loose my temper, turn to tornado,
    I agree, ambitious and acrid am I,
I beg forgiveness for devil deeds,
    Within wet winds, I weep and cry.

{45} *Canadian Summer*

Why summer is so short lived,
I feel the emptiness around,
Branches ashamed of naked trees,
Leaves have fallen on the ground.

Flowers, their glowing petals,
Are mixed with dust and sand,
Only thorns are left behind,
The greenery has left the land.

Open arms of wind have swept,
Everything that came their way,
Thunder cries down the sky,
Youth of summer is taken away.

But there is hope, life will return,
Meadows will turn green again,
Colourful flowers will blossom,
And things will reappear same.

Meenakshi Raina

{46} *Complex Equations*

Some complex equations of life,
don't have a solution, but a lesson
for us to comprehend and ponder.

We are a result of the choices we
make, decisions we take and the
way we handle the situations in life.

Equations of life are not made of
numbers, but formed by our attitude
and opinions that we carry with us.

Find that common factor of love and
reduce expectations to zero, it might
change the complex dynamics of life.

For unsolved equations add some trust,
subtract hate, multiply with care and
leave that hidden fraction of arrogance.

Some equations do have a limitation
some have a variable solution, the key
lies in balancing out the equations of life.

{47} Your Memories

It is not the loneliness but
your memories that hurt me most.

Distances, try to keep us apart,
but your love resides in my heart,
The memories take away my peace,
I find my heartbeat trying to cease.
It is not the loneliness but
your memories that hurt me most.

My silence will burn me from inside,
and my love for you I can't hide,
When I breathe your memories,
they lock me with you and then freeze.
It is not the loneliness but
your memories that hurt me most.

The garden chair, memories it brings,
my lonesome heart weeps and sings,
But I can't stop thinking of you again,
and memories of you, bring me pain.
It is not the loneliness but
your memories that hurt me most.

{48} She Waited

She waited and waited for many decades,
She watched the door and never bolted,
She went alone to places in his search,
She wrote letters but never posted.

Her lover never came, her youth was lost,
Too many wrinkles, time slowly left,
Perhaps death alone would bring her peace,
She waited for love, now waited for death.

She closed her eyes and pretended dead,
But death vanished when her eyes opened,
She read the unposted letters she wrote,
And her innocent tears got them soaked.

The only night she bolted the door,
She heard a knock again and again,
Collecting her senses she couldn't judge,
If it was love or death ready to embrace.

{49} *In Deep Sorrow*

With three bullets in my chest
You thought I wouldn't live on
In shock your heartbeats calmed
You died, but I survived.

War is over, but each day I battle life
How shall I live without you?
You were my hope and my dream
Now all I have is emptiness.

Buried are you, but not your love
It shall live in my memories
My heart now bruises with regrets
Certain things shall remain unsaid.

As I close my eyes to feel you
Tears descend to rest on your tomb
While winds whisper your name
Life without you will not be same.

To honour your life and love for me
I leave flowers on cold stone
And as I walk away from you
In deep sorrow, I keep looking behind.

For sure, our souls shall unite
The day we meet in unknown land.

{50} *When Flowers Basked In Sunlight*

Clouds had melted and sun was shining bright
harmony in garden sun's rays did bring,
Roses were shy, daisies danced in delight.

Sunflowers waved at sun, what a great sight
their petals were perfectly placed in ring,
Clouds had melted and sun was shining bright.

Lilies felt drowsy had not slept last night
silently admired sun, didn't say a thing,
Roses were shy, daisies danced in delight.

Calm breeze swayed the flowers from left to right
flowers bloomed, butterflies began to cling,
Clouds had melted and sun was shining bright.

Purple pansies peeped as they had small height
range of colours held the elegant spring,
Roses were shy, daisies danced in delight.

Flowers were excited, basked in sunlight
while swarming bees stopped by, started to sing,
Clouds had melted and sun was shining bright,
Roses were shy, daisies danced in delight.

{51} *Unkind Autumn*

Roaring winds swirl the brittle leaves,
Undressed and cold stand tenuous trees.
Birds silently sing a mournful song,
Curtains of clouds are thick and long.

Immutable wheel of time moves on,
Stunning spring and summer are gone.
Pain and unrest, are intertwined,
Autumn regrets for being unkind.

In every leaf, in every bare tree,
Sorrow soars autumn steals their glee.
Formidable storms sweep gardens glow,
And whisk the roses from every row.

Spring is far, with winter interlude,
Bereft of green robes, earth stays nude.
Smearing the clouds sun demurely peeps,
Why sketch of sadness autumn seeks?

{52} *Longing*

Will you be my companion?
In the journey of my life,
Will you be there for me?
In the journey of my life.

I want to colour the rainbow,
With the colours of our love,
I want to fly up in the sky,
With the wings of our trust.

I want to live my life,
With your dreams to fill it,
I want to follow you,
On your imprints left behind.

I want to grow old with you,
With the years of togetherness,
I want to create memories with you,
In the journey of my life.

{53} *Letting Go*

Let there be no memories of you
Even the ones those are almost new
They remind me false promises and lies
Trust is now over with tears in my eyes
I give up on you and let myself free
Never thought this could happen to me
Goodbye didn't come easy it was hard

Grief and regret soon shall be barred
Only peace my healing heart shall guard

You left and I waited without clue,
Maybe our love wasn't meant to thrive,
Nothing stops life and I forgive you,
For my heart to breathe and survive.

I buried the past
forgiveness gave a new start
life is beautiful.

{54} Spring Rain

Spring rain comes
dancing on ground
it seeps through
cracks of dry land
heals the wounds
and buds bloom
    Raw rain drops
    stay quiet on leaves
    and dribble on
    nest beneath where
    love birds swing
    enjoy the patter
Brave breeze opens
red tulip buds
sunrays give kiss
they feel shy and
bend towards wet
shade of trees
    Bluebirds sing
    the tune of spring
    I calmly listen
    and miss grandma
    who used to keep
    grains for hungry birds

{55} *Summer Sun*

Sun, sand and seashore
sky in blue meadows in green
splendid summer shines

placed row after row
the obedient flowers
praise the summer sun

{56} *Toxic State*

Bullets wrapped in death
　　Hitting the frame of life
　　　Humanity left with no breath,
Shadow of love holds knife
　　Peace has dissolved in hate
　　　Dark and dangerous is life,
Tears trickle down my eyes
　　World is in a toxic state
　　　Unable to filter truth and lies.

Meenakshi Raina

{57} *Nothing Else Matters*

I feel your breath, still frightened to death,
But as long as, I have faith in my prayers.
Nothing else matters.

The rivals don't know, the power of mother,
Who stands by you, who loves and cares.
Nothing else matters.

You are safe in my arms, open your eyes,
Let me kiss your forehead, wipe your tears.
Nothing else matters.

I shall shield you, from devil's dark shadow,
I believe your say, not what said by others.
Nothing else matters.

World is evil, I am afraid of your innocence,
But I will make you strong, in coming years.
Nothing else matters.

Trust me for once, you are my reason to live,
Wake up my child, and give me all your fears.
Nothing else matters.

{58} You Are My Queen

Before I met you, my life was autumn leaf,
Shadows followed me, my life was in grief,
Withered and wasted without your love,
You came in my life, blessing from above.

In the story of my life, you are my queen,
So never leave me, lovely my life has been.

Our days are few, time went away and flew,
I know how lonely life can be without you,
I no longer steer in my old memory lanes,
They bring emotional pain, drive me insane.

In the story of my life, you are my queen,
So never leave me, lovely my life has been.

{59} *Before He Sets My Soul Free*

I believe He is an artist at heart
and his creations are a marvellous art
the birth
of earth
ball in blue and green is art full of worth

I believe He is a great magician
He sparkled sky with stars, moon and sun
to light
to bright
and end darkness that bothers the night

I believe He can read our mind
though He is invisible, no one can find
He is everywhere
to take our care
listens and answers our sincere prayer

I believe He is the life, He is the death
He is the one who rules every breath
what I see
infinite is He
of this mystical universe He has the key

Before He sets my soul free
A noble person I want to be!

{60} *You Stole My Heart*

Outside the city where the pomegranates grow,
There you stole my heart and I didn't even know,
Under the shade of tall trees in the green land,
You looked in my blue eyes and held my hand

I think of you, though far away thousand miles,
It is so hard to forget the charm of your smile,
Outside the city where the pomegranates grow,
There you stole my heart and I didn't even know

In my dream I saw you waiting with open arms,
And I came running passing the barn and farms,
Outside the city where the pomegranates grow,
There you stole my heart and I didn't even know

The magic of your love has changed me so much,
Sometimes falling leaves make me feel your touch,
Outside the city where the pomegranates grow,
There you stole my heart and I didn't even know.

{61} *Love Is Actually Magical*

When seeds of emptiness no longer survive,
With force of faith, heart is no more skeptical,
When silence sinks and soft beats of love arrive,
I know love is actually magical.

Eternal is love, my flimsy heart shall thrive,
I believe wonders of love are whimsical.
Stones of sorrow shall silently crush to sand,
Yes, true love secretly holds magical wand.

{62} *Why I Love Solitude*

Solitude, takes me to the river of imagination
where, ideas ripple and words in rhythm float.
With patience, I ponder and pursue my thoughts,
some are vague, some plain and some with pain,
I add some emotions, dress them in words,
and the ornaments of rhyme decorate my thoughts.
So, when peace of mind pairs with my passion,
and when pen and paper collide, a poem is born,
Without solitude I am too normal but to reach
out to the poet in me, all I desire is solitude.
It takes me away from the maddening crowd,
and I enjoy the magnificence of being alone.

{63} *Real Love*

Love is nothing but an emotion of soul,
Love when selfless, reward is not the goal.

It wasn't easy to fall in love without trust,
With uneasy heart slowly I tried to adjust.

Trust came first long before I loved you,
And with passing time my love slowly grew.

Love brought hope, hope of togetherness,
It united our hearts with feeling of oneness.

Life had challenges nothing came straight,
Your love made me strong to fight the fate.

I found in you, real love that I longed for,
In my dark life you came like a bright star.

Life is beautiful with your precious love,
Blessed I feel with no regrets in life now.

Love is spring sunshine with gentle breeze,
And without your love my life would cease.

Years gone by, in reality our love is still new,
As again and again, I fall in love with you.

{64} *Garden Of Remembrance*

And the cemetery was a garden of remembrance,
to honour those who left world, found a new abode,
And their families grieved, missed the loved ones,
with moist eyes, and their hearts entirely sorrowed.

She prayed for hours, close to her beloved's grave,
cleaned the fallen leaves, cleared the tousled vines,
She let those tears fall and found them hard to save,
yet again she recalled that fatal day, and his last lines.

Beside her beloved's grave, plucked the only flower,
and kissed it with her closed eyes, felt the fragrance,
She believed the rose carried the smile of her lover,
and he watched her from above, she felt his presence.

Before she left his cold grave, one last time she cried,
why destiny had snatched him untimely, she sighed,
She never got a chance in life to be his wedded bride,
the cemetery had many stories of love buried inside.

{65} *Kashmir*

Kashmir! Heavenly grace,
Endless beauty to behold,
Saints, sages found solace,
Eternal- their verses of gold.

Peace and destiny on strife,
And fugitives were bold,
There began a run for life,
In white winter, wild and cold.

Bloodshed, the lost kith and kin,
Story of pain, remained untold,
Why they paid for other's sin?
Thoughts have pined, tears rolled.

{66} Mind Has Its Own Cabins

Mind has
its own cabins,
where we can find
love, hate, anger,
happiness and
much more.

All emotions
can't fit in one,
they are complex,
and tend to have,
their own cabins,
where they thrive.

It is up to you
how many good
and bad cabins,
you want your
mind to allocate
and handle.

Clean the cabins
with negativity,
put away the burden,
and keep them
for things that
matter you most.

{67} No More Tears

Yesterday your tear drop fell on my table
And it created storm in the ocean of my love,
As long as I live, no more tears for you
Save them for the time when death takes me away,
My love for you is enough to wipe your sorrow
On my table... today I left flowers for you.

{68} Wrapped In Silence

Grandma couldn't
speak for weeks,
Speech left her,
even before her soul.
She would stare
at empty walls,
Perhaps saw death
waiting at door.

Before she
breathed her last,
Her eyes held
questions, no tears.
She struggled to
say her last words,
As they came
wrapped in silence.

Those last words,
remain a mystery,
Will never know,
what she had to say.

{69} *Shades Of Love*

Hand in hand, we walk on lush green carpet
towards the grey shadows of emerald trees
where we can avoid, golden eyes of sun that are on us.

A pair of brown sparrows with yellow beaks is singing
it seems they are in love too as they ignored us completely
and took their flight with their wings entwined.

Far away from crowded city life, I breathe freedom,
I love this moment while I am walking with you and
I enjoy peace and the different shades of love you bring.

Though the white clouds are chasing the blue sky,
I wish the silver rain drops could fall, to make us wet
and I would hold you closer beneath my purple umbrella.

{70} Where Will They Find

I will never be completely gone,
My love, you will find me -
in your beautiful memories,
in our daughter's subtle smile,
in places where we have fun,
in walls holding my picture,
in dry roses saved in wooden box,
in things we like to do together,
in the mirror that looks at me,
in the verses I write for you,
in the books I hold close to heart,
in the spilled dry ink on my table that
I left like that, as it made a great art.

{71} *The Last Call*

My worst fear is what if
I die a sudden death,
where unexpectedly I am
deprived of my breath.
    I want death to be kind
    approach in steps small,
    and when I hear them louder
    I know it is the last call.
A similar wish to God
my grandma also made,
I heard her many times
when sincerely she prayed.
    Fortunate was my grandma
    now I keep wishing on a star,
    and I hope God listens to
    what I fear for.
Death is the ultimate truth
and life has to descend,
I don't want my loved ones
to face my abrupt end.

{72} *Introspection*

I illuminate myself with silence, listen to inner voice
Nurture my mind with positive energy and hope
Take some time to influence myself towards my goal
Ruminate on my actions, and strive for perfection
Outline my weak points, challenge myself to overcome
Self-examination gives me input needed for progress
Purifying mind, removing clutter of negative thoughts
Emerging with a desire to be better than yesterday
Correcting myself, bad choices are learning for future
Turning to my inner-self and searching answers
Into the mine of my soul I dig deep and contemplate
Once I overcome my inhibition and know my strengths
Nothing is impossible, I believe in myself and stay focused

Meenakshi Raina

{73} *Sweet Little Lies*

Those sweet little lies
Why didn't I realize.

My love for you was pure
but you tried to ignore
I should have known before
and closed my heart's door.

Those sweet little lies
Why didn't I realize.

Your laugh and your love
both were a black dove
don't want to trust you now
as you broke your vow.

Those sweet little lies
Why didn't I realize.

Countless times I cried
what if you hadn't lied
I would be your side
Our love would have survived.

Those sweet little lies
Why didn't I realize.

{74} *Unspoken Words*

Sometimes unspoken words,
Make graves in our heart,
We carry their heavy burden,
And they never decide to part.

I held the unspoken words,
Got hopeless regrets and sorrow,
I wonder, without letting me know,
How did the regrets slowly grow?

Sometimes breaking the silence,
Is the hardest thing, takes forever,
Why didn't I trust unspoken words?
And set them free for better.

Let the grudges meet an end,
Let the regrets be now dead,
Let the words flow at their pace,
Let the unspoken be now said.

{75} *Being Human*

Believe in yourself, empathise with others and undertake acts of kindness.

Endorse humility and compassion, and unite to curb the roots of evil forces.

In today's world where violence shadows the peace, we mainly depend on

Nurturing righteousness and uphold the human values that differentiate

Good from bad, right from wrong and let our conscience be untainted.

Honour life, foster harmony around us and help those who need our support.

Ultimately what makes us different from animals is our human instinct.

Mistakes are to be taken as lessons learnt, have faith and hope for the best.

Acknowledge the fact - live and let others live, life is precious, life is short

Nothing lives forever, only our acts of kindness are left behind in the world.

{76} You Won't

you won't know my pain
   when silent tears mix with rain
      get washed without being seen

you won't hear my voice
   when cold cries mix with loud noise
      I cling alone to my woes

you won't see my love
   when time mixes with money
      there are no memories made

Meenakshi Raina

{77} *Tiny Tears*

Fill my life with colours of love,
Let me forget the woes from past,
Entice me with your magic now,
Fill my life with colours of love,
Give me desire to live somehow,
Embrace this moment, it won't last,
Fill my life with colours of love,
Let me forget the woes from past.

Wipe away tiny tears of gloom,
Hope you be my eternal spring,
Garden of my life failed to bloom,
Wipe away tiny tears of gloom,
Silence heaved me in vacuum,
Solace your courteous words bring,
Wipe away tiny tears of gloom,
Hope you be my eternal spring.

{78} *Abandoned Houses*

The old abandoned houses in Kashmir,
Do wonder where did the families go,
Although it happened long, long ago.

If for once houses were allowed to talk,
They would share their stories of pain,
How much they waited, to see us again.

If like us they would hold the memories,
They would talk about the happier days,
When happiness came in numerous ways.

They would talk about celebrations in past,
The customs, rituals that were followed,
But, now life inside them had hollowed.

Vacant houses, testify terror and trauma,
They know every bit of bitter truth,
Their invisible heart too, was hurt in youth.

For two decades they didn't hear laughter,
No one peeped through their windows,
Their glory was lost, like hapless widows.

They stand mute waiting for death,
Their broken walls can't hold roof above,
They may only live few years from now.

Meenakshi Raina

{79} *And I Saunter Alone*

Morning breeze whispers, winter is here,
And I welcome the first snowfall.

Who shaped the snowflakes and painted them white,
Silent are secrets of sky,
And I saunter alone.

Icicles hanging from naked branches,
Some of them like meandering around,
Creating a wonderful gleaming art,
While some eagerly wait to touch the ground.

Cold sunrays emerge,
Shiny snow, pure and peaceful,
White blanket coats land,
I find some unknown footprints,
And I miss warmth, your love brings.

{80} *River Of Love*

Words of kindness untainted and soft like dove,
Stole my sorrows, replaced them with hope now,
When mountains of sadness touched river of love,
My solitude melted away, woes couldn't last,

Wrapped by your love, I no more reside in past,
And wild wounds from betrayal healed so fast,
Your love came like luster in darkness so vast,
You wiped my tears, and gave me a fresh start,

We were destined to unite, shall never part,
The song of love chanted by your holy heart,
Runs deep in my soul, mystical is your art,
I no longer wish for diamonds or gold,

Your love is enough my heart silently told,
Smiles are my jewels, loneliness got sold,
Now my regrets from life are faded and cold,
I pray for you to be safe from evil eye,

With you I dream to touch silver stars in sky,
You are my wings of hope, help me to fly,
Love gave- flowers of faith money couldn't buy,
Words of kindness untainted and soft like dove.

{81} *My Plea*

Oh God! Alienate me from foes, dissipate me from vice,
Gravitate me to righteousness make me noble and wise.

In this malignant world with savage and inurbane minds,
Life has become hostile and peace is hard to find.

Please forgive me, for I may sound capricious sometimes,
I don't know how to flatter or praise You, in my poems.

Give me courage, I am lost like a scapegoat in wilderness,
Transitory is life, bestow me light take away the darkness.

In my perspicuous plea, all I want is sorrows to end,
Show me the right path that leads to you, for me to blend.

{82} *Overgrown Vines*

Silence had consumed him, since the time
she left for eternal peace and now she only
visited him in his dreams.

With headstone covered with moss and
overgrown vines he couldn't believe that
too many years passed in loneliness.

Her carved name was hardly visible even
in bright sunlight, but he recognized her
final place of rest.

Vines were in love with her too, he thought,
they earnestly held her headstone with
their tangled arms.

He felt no fear, left her in their care, in sun
and rain, as he knew they were there while
she rested in peace.

A twig from a vine, he used as pen and wrote
on the headstone covered with green moss -
'remembering you on our fiftieth wedding anniversary'.

{83} *Nostalgic Snow*

When I watch snow, it isn't just white,
It recounts my colourful childhood,
Spent in lap of mesmerising Kashmir,
Memories still alive, fresh and good.

When I watch snow, it isn't just quite,
It echoes the voices from my past,
Mother's yell, insisting to be inside,
While I built snowman in cold blast.

When I watch snow, it isn't just polite,
It reveals hidden secrets of snow fight,
Throwing snowballs big and small,
While stars watched in the dark night.

Why was I thrown out of my homeland?
Nostalgic snow, makes my eyes wet,
Memories, get unleashed by snowflakes,
And keep my past alive, lest I forget.

{84} Seeds Of Peace

The band of flowers,
Arranged in a wreath,
Were wrapped in woe,
And immersed in grief.

The wreath was laid,
To respect the Martyr,
Cupped petals cried,
And saluted his valour.

He combated enemies,
Followed the command,
And sacrificed his life,
For his motherland.

Are enemies ashamed,
Of their wicked deeds?
The seeds of peace,
Is what the world needs.

Let the humanity win,
Let the weapons fail,
Let the hatred vanish,
Let the peace prevail.

{85} *Camouflaged Opportunities*

Chance, choice and circumstances can create,
new opportunities in life, to change our fate.
Some challenges camouflage opportunities ahead,
give a thought, don't discard them and shred.
Take different view of situations and think over,
could be golden opportunity, may not return ever.
Spot and seize opportunities, they are success keys,
don't let them wait, act fast, no time to sit at ease.
Sometimes hidden opportunities pretend like threats,
they come and they go, missed ones leave regrets.
Life itself is an opportunity, to strive for the best,
try to fulfill your dreams, with vigour and zest.

{86} Nothingness

My path of life was full of thorns,
she covered it with her velvet smile,

When I silently embraced loneliness,
she walked beside me hand in hand,

When my shadow questioned my worth,
she answered and calmed the unrest,

I burned my dreams, she saved ashes,
I cursed my fate, she believed in God,

When hope had left, she gave faith,
and saved my life from nothingness.

{87} *Wonderful Beauty In White*

Full moon shining bright, beautiful is night,
And dancing snowflakes quietly touch me.
Immersed in moonlight, the snowflakes glow,
And I wonder how beautiful, white could be.

Magnificent mountains covered with snow,
Roaming clouds, hiding their pointed peaks.
Rocks too carefully wrapped in white wear,
While I stand silent, glorious beauty speaks.

Open fields in spotless white, calm and quiet,
Bare trees are shy, though icicles drape branches.
Serene white, is what winter decided to bring,
Wonderful beauty, from above even He watches.

{88} *Future*

Future is far like a cloud in sky,
Wings of hope will take me high,

Dreams are the seeds of future,
Will sow them with love and care,

I wonder what the future brings,
I wish I could foresee the things,

Though future is a story untold,
Slowly its mysteries will unfold,

I bury the past, it is now dead,
Let my focus be on future ahead.

Meenakshi Raina

{89} Ribbons And Bows

Ribbons and bows tied to the flames
   Sparkling fireworks touch the sky,
Silver stars show shimmering smile
   And I wish my loneliness goodbye.

Ashes of regrets have blown away
   Colourful flames rewarded delight,
I no more sink in painful memories
   Sparks of joy, have filled the night.

Flames of forgiveness, I embraced
   And my heart has learnt to survive,
I cherish my life and celebrate
   Heat of desires shall keep me alive.

{90} *Paradise Lost*

P oisonous minds roamed in Valley of joy,
A nd their mission was to kill and destroy.
R uthless bullets pierced the innocent hearts,
A ngry devils tried to tear the Valley apart.
D eath danced every street, none could flee,
I struggled to breathe, as fear consumed me.
S ilently, world watched attack on humanity,
E ven weather was merciless in Jan of 1990.

L eft my land to survive in unknown place,
O nly hope I carried, to march in life's race.
S o many years gone, Valley still screams,
T oday Kashmir is safe only in my dreams.

Acknowledgements

We always curse the darkness but it is the darkness that led me to the path of poetry. Sounds strange, but it is true! During my childhood years in Kashmir there used to be constant power outages in night and sometimes even for hours together. We would light up a candle or an oil lamp or stay in the dark.

My mother would recite the poems of famous poets in Hindi language. She would also give me one-liners and I would come up with a rhyming second line. Sometimes she would select topics from everyday life and I would share my thoughts; that is how I got introduced to creative writing. I would like to thank my mother Usha Kashkari for being my guru and for polishing my skills in Hindi poetry which has helped me in making my way in English poetry.

My gratitude goes to my publisher, Bala Menon of Tamarind Tree Books of Toronto, for making this book happen.

I would like to thank Vijay Kurup for the book design and illustration on page 14.

A big thank you to Sudhir Anand of the Voice Media Group (The Weekly Voice, Punjabi Awaaz, Radio Voice, VNN - Voice News Network and www.weeklyvoice.com), for his valuable guidance.

My sincere thanks to Dr. Azad Kaushik for his encouragement and moral support.

Many thanks to my sisters – Kamakshi Vaidya and Ojasvi Kaul for being my first readers and believing in me.

I would like to express my utmost gratitude to George Elliott Clarke (Parliamentary Poet Laureate of Canada

{Contd.} *Acknowledgements*

2016-17) for reading some of my poems and expressing his thoughts in a supporting paragraph for my book.

I would like to thank my wonderful family for their love and support throughout the making of this book and for being patient for the whole time. Special thanks to my husband Sunny Raina for dealing with my poetic tantrums and to my daughter Divena Raina for being a great listener.

Earlier versions of some of these poems have appeared in the following publications and websites: 'Incredible Indo-Canadians' souvenir / magazine by National Alliance of Indo-Canadians, www.shehjar.com, www.poetrysoup.com, thank you to their respective editors.

Last, but not the least, I would like to thank the Markham Public Library, Ontario, Canada, for lending their vast collection of poetry books that helped me in developing my writing skills.

About The Author

Meenakshi Raina is a Canada-based author and a Kashmiri Pandit. Her debut historical fiction *'The Divine And The Destiny'* is based on the mass exodus of Kashmiri Pandits in 1990. She is also a contributing author for the recently published non-fiction *'A Long Dream of Home'*.

Meenakshi was born in Jammu but lived her childhood years in Kashmir Valley.

After the turmoil in the Valley in 1990, she migrated to Jammu and did her graduation in science from Camp College, Jammu and her post-graduation, Master of Management Studies (M.M.S) from University of Mumbai.

She qualified the UGC, NET (National Educational Test) for Lecturership and also worked as a lecturer in India.

She migrated to Canada in the year 2001 and lives with her husband in Toronto, Canada. Since her childhood, writing poems has been her passion in both Hindi and English languages.

'Far In The Meadows' is her debut poetry collection.

www.ingramcontent.com/pod-product-compliance
Lightning Source LLC
Chambersburg PA
CBHW031313060726
47590CB00003B/1188